JELLYFISH

LIFE CYCLES

Words that look like **this** can be found in the glossary on page 24.

BookLife
PUBLISHING

©2019
BookLife Publishing Ltd.
King's Lynn
Norfolk PE30 4LS

A catalogue record for this book is available from the British Library.

ISBN: 978-1-78637-735-7

Written by:
Shalini Vallepur

Edited by:
William Anthony

Designed by:
Danielle Jones

All facts, statistics, web addresses and URLs in this book were verified as valid and accurate at time of writing.
No responsibility for any changes to external websites or references can be accepted by either the author or publisher.

CONTENTS

WHAT IS A LIFE CYCLE?

All animals, plants and humans go through different stages of their life as they grow and change. This is called a life cycle.

Human life cycle

Baby  **Child**  **Adult**

WHAT IS A JELLYFISH?

Jellyfish are a type of **invertebrate**. Adult jellyfish are bell-shaped and have **tentacles** that can cause a painful sting.

Tentacles

A group of jellyfish is called a smack.

EGGS

Female jellyfish can release up to 45,000 eggs per day. Male jellyfish **fertilise** the eggs.

Jellyfish egg

The eggs float in the ocean water while they **develop**.
Soon, they will be ready to hatch.

After laying
their eggs,
females swim
away and leave
them forever.

PLANULA LARVAE

The eggs hatch into planula larvae. They are tiny and covered in hairs called cilia. The cilia help to move the larvae through the water.

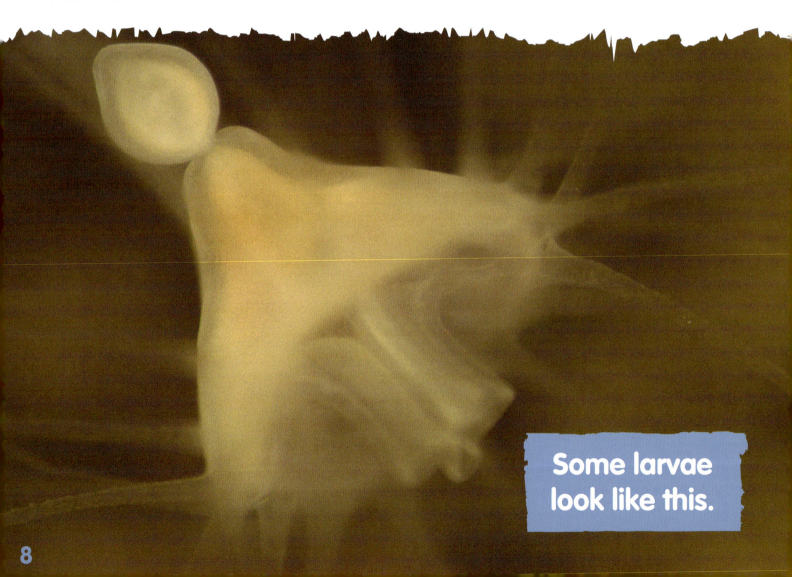

Some larvae look like this.

The larvae float down and attach themselves to a hard <u>surface</u>. The larvae will stay there for a long time.

Rocks are a perfect place for larvae to settle.

POLYPS

Once they're on the ground, the larvae turn into polyps. Polyps look like stalks. They have tentacles and a mouth at the top.

Plankton

Polyps feed on plankton.

A polyp stays in the same place and grows for many years. It grows new polyps and becomes a **colony**.

This is a crown jellyfish polyp colony.

JELLYFISH

The stalks of the polyps turn into tiny, young jellyfish.
They can be as small as two millimetres wide.

This polyp is turning into a jellyfish.

Over a few weeks, the young jellyfish get bigger and become fully grown adults.

A young jellyfish is called an ephyra.

Jellyfish are **carnivores**. They use their long tentacles to sting small fish and crabs before eating them.

An adult jellyfish is called a medusa.

When the jellyfish are big enough, they are ready to reproduce. This starts the life cycle again.

TYPES OF JELLYFISH

There are 2,000 different **species** of jellyfish and they are found all over the world. They come in lots of different colours and sizes.

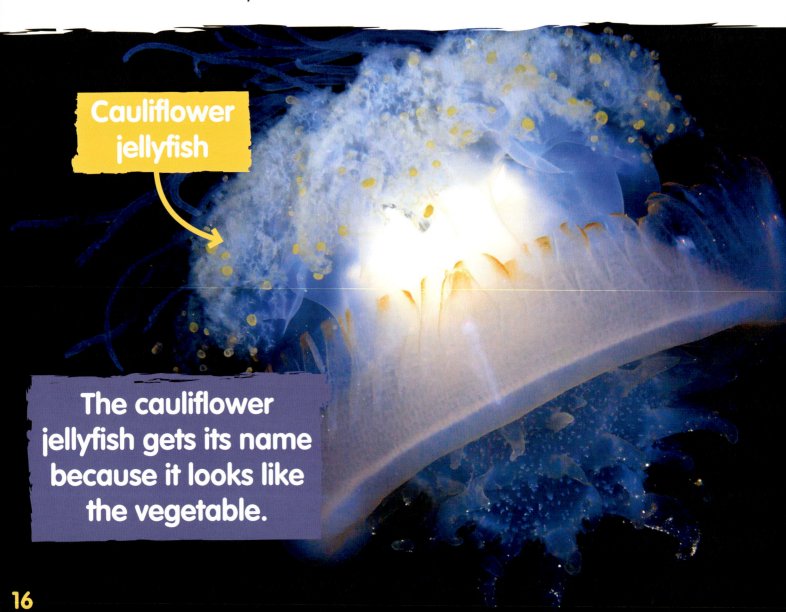

Cauliflower jellyfish

The cauliflower jellyfish gets its name because it looks like the vegetable.

Fried egg jellyfish

The fried egg jellyfish's colours make it look just like a fried egg!
Its tentacles can grow up to six metres long.

JELLYFISH FACTS

Jellyfish are believed to have been around for 500 million years. Jellyfish **fossils** tell us that jellyfish have been on our planet for a very long time.

Some jellyfish can glow in the dark. The crystal jellyfish's body is see-through and it can make light.

Some people think this confuses its <u>predators</u>.

WORLD RECORD BREAKERS

Longest Jellyfish

The longest jellyfish in the world is the lion's mane jellyfish. It can grow up to 36 metres long. It has around 800 tentacles to catch **prey**.

Deadliest Sting

The box jellyfish has the most dangerous sting of any jellyfish. It can be found near Australia.

LIFE CYCLE OF A JELLYFISH

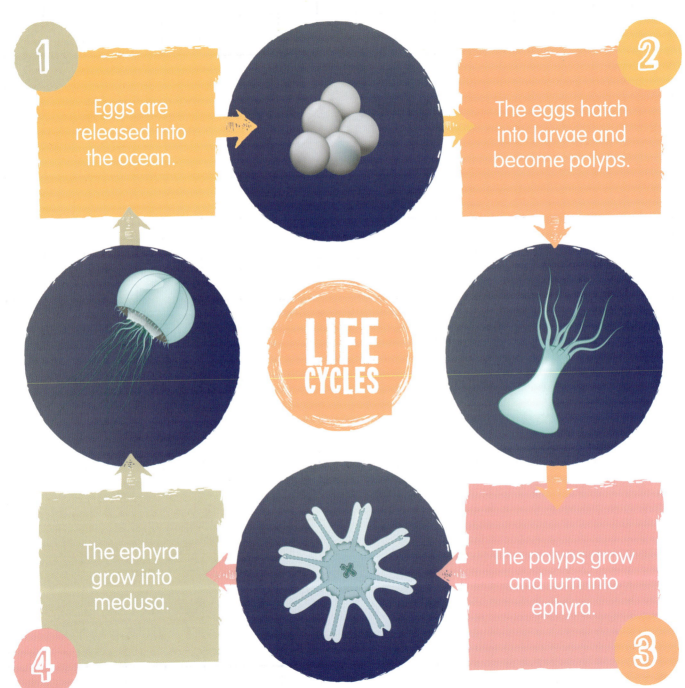

1 Eggs are released into the ocean.

2 The eggs hatch into larvae and become polyps.

3 The polyps grow and turn into ephyra.

4 The ephyra grow into medusa.

LIFE CYCLES

GET EXPLORING!

Have you ever seen a jellyfish? Visit a local aquarium to learn more about these fantastic creatures.

GLOSSARY

carnivores	animals that eat other animals rather than plants
colony	a group of plants or animals living or growing in one place
develop	when something grows or changes
fertilise	to cause an egg to develop into a new living thing
fossils	the remains of a living animal or plant from a very long time ago, set in rock
invertebrate	an animal that does not have a backbone
plankton	microscopic creatures that float in the sea
predators	animals that hunt other animals for food
prey	animals that are hunted by other animals for food
species	a group of very similar animals or plants that can produce young together
surface	the outside of something, such as a rock
tentacles	long thin body parts that are used to feel or hold things

INDEX